POP PIANO HITS

SIMPLE ARRANGEMENTS FOR STUDENTS

Blank Space, I Really Like You & More Hot Singles

ISBN 978-1-4950-2327-9

HAL•LEONARD®
CORPORATION
7777 W. BLUEMOUND RD. P.O. BOX 13819 MILWAUKEE, WI 53213

Visit Hal Leonard Online at
www.halleonard.com

Contents

BLANK SPACE

Words and Music by TAYLOR SWIFT,
MAX MARTIN and SHELLBACK

Moderately slow

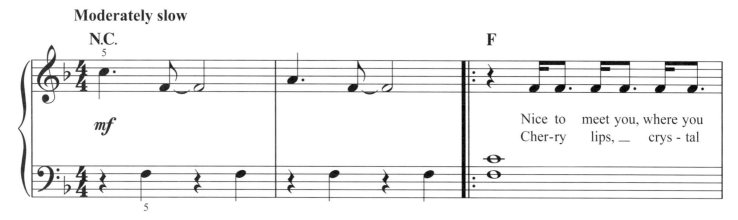

Nice to meet you, where you
Cher-ry lips, __ crys-tal

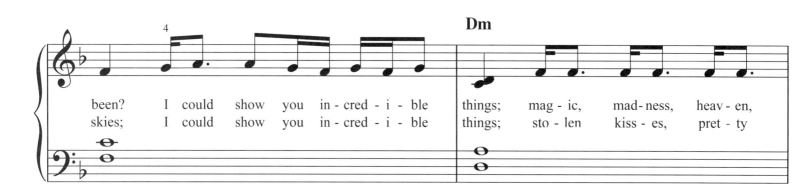

been? I could show you in-cred-i-ble things; mag-ic, mad-ness, heav-en,
skies; I could show you in-cred-i-ble things; sto-len kiss-es, pret-ty

sin. Saw you there, and I ___ thought, "Oh my God. Look at that face!
lies. You're the king, ba-by. I'm your queen. Find out what __ you want.

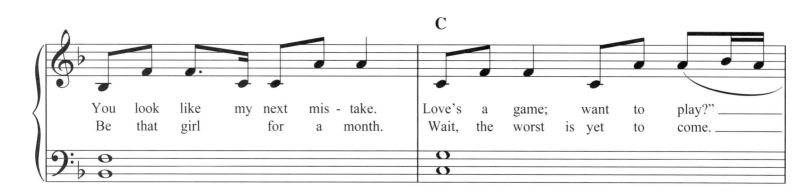

You look like my next mis-take. Love's a game; want to play?" ___
Be that girl for a month. Wait, the worst is yet to come. ___

F

Eh.
Oh.

New mon - ey, suit and
Scream - ing, cry - ing, per - fect

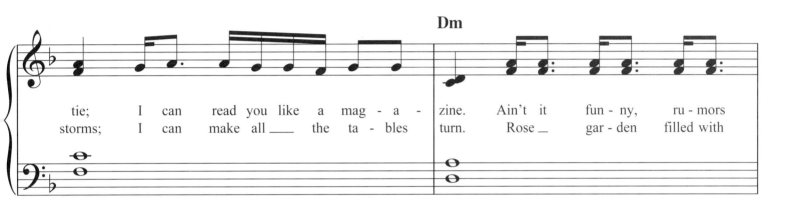

Dm

tie; I can read you like a mag - a - zine. Ain't it fun - ny, ru - mors
storms; I can make all ___ the ta - bles turn. Rose ___ gar - den filled with

Bb

fly, and I know you heard a - bout me. So hey, let's be friends. I'm
thorns; keep you sec - ond guess - ing like: "Oh my God, who is she?"

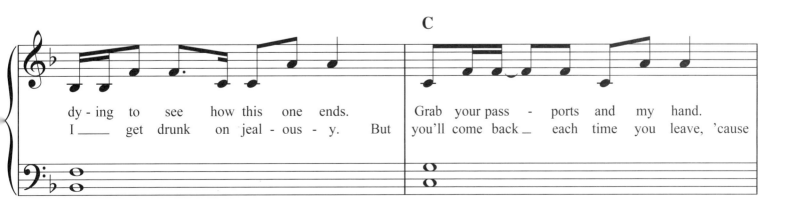

C

dy - ing to see how this one ends.
I ___ get drunk on jeal - ous - y. But

Grab your pass - ports and my hand.
you'll come back ___ each time you leave, 'cause

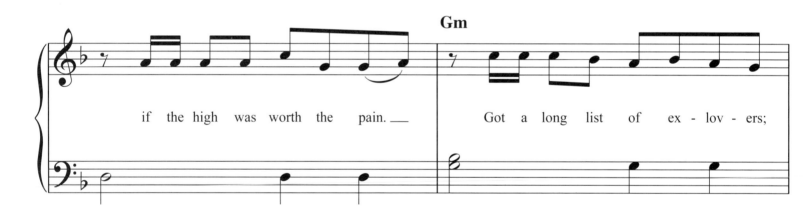

and you love the game. 'Cause we're young and we're reck - less,

we'll take this way too far. ___ It -'ll leave you breath-less, mm, or with a nas - ty scar. ___

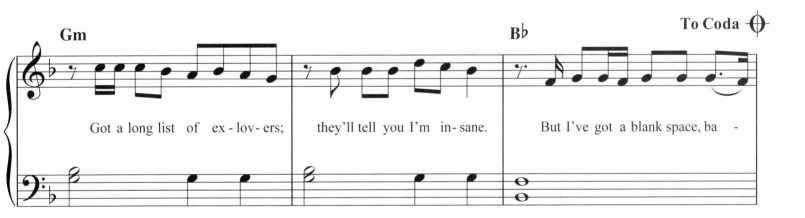

Got a long list of ex - lov - ers; they'll tell you I'm in - sane. But I've got a blank space, ba -

To Coda ⊕

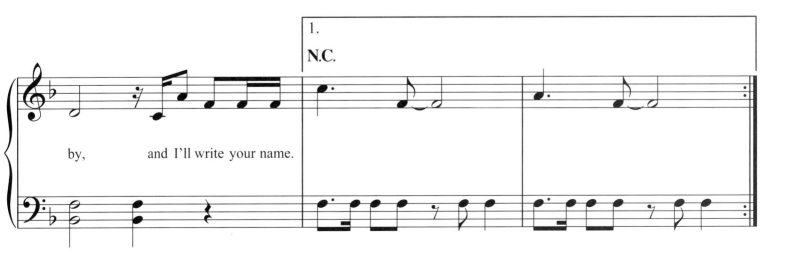

1.

N.C.

by, and I'll write your name.

Boys on-ly want love if it's tor - ture. Don't say I did-n't,

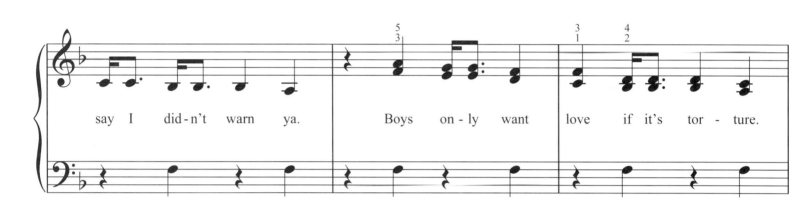

say I did-n't warn ya. Boys on-ly want love if it's tor - ture.

D.S. al Coda

Don't say I did - n't, say I did - n't warn ya.

CODA

by, and I'll write your name.

I'M NOT THE ONLY ONE

Words and Music by SAM SMITH
and JAMES NAPIER

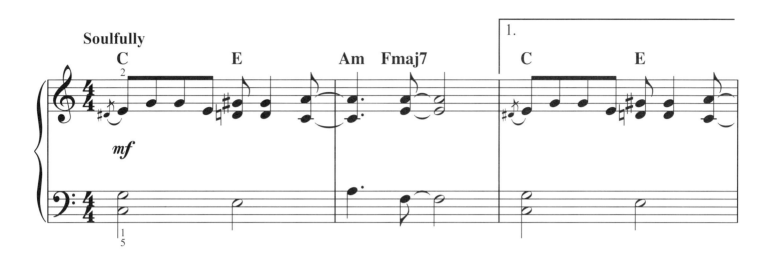

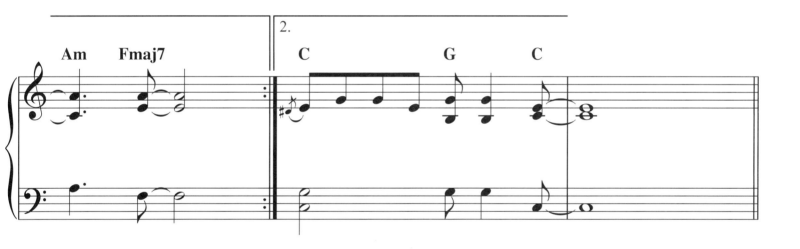

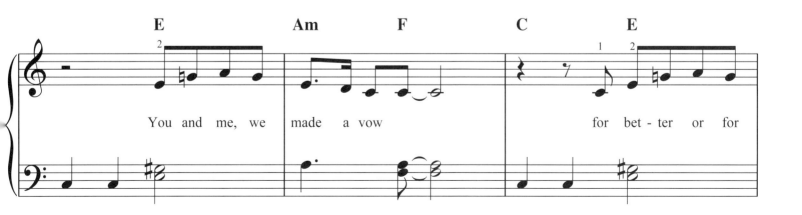

You and me, we made a vow for bet-ter or for

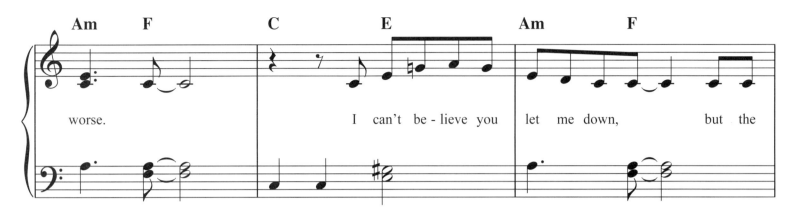

worse. I can't be-lieve you let me down, but the

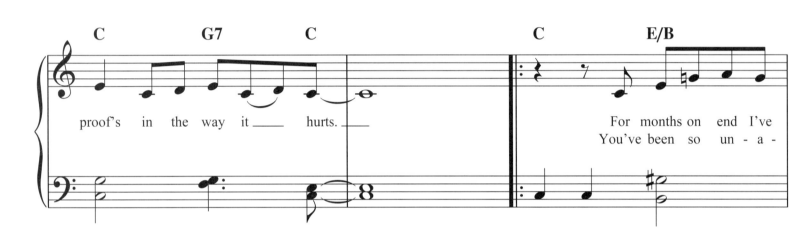

proof's in the way it _____ hurts. _____

For months on end I've
You've been so un-a-

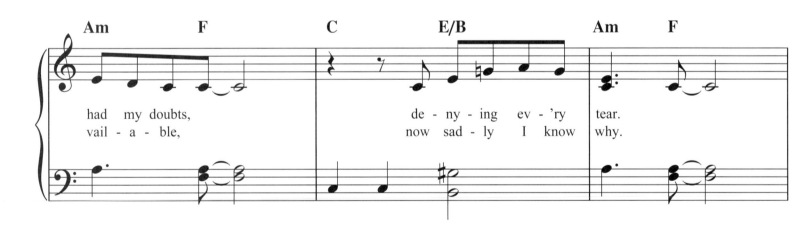

had my doubts,
vail - a - ble,

de - ny - ing ev - 'ry tear.
now sad - ly I know why.

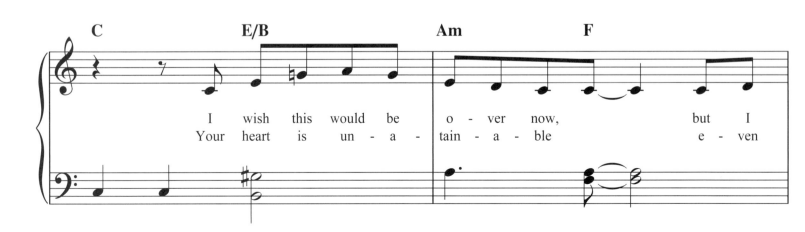

I wish this would be
Your heart is un-a-

o - ver now,
tain - a - ble

but I
e - ven

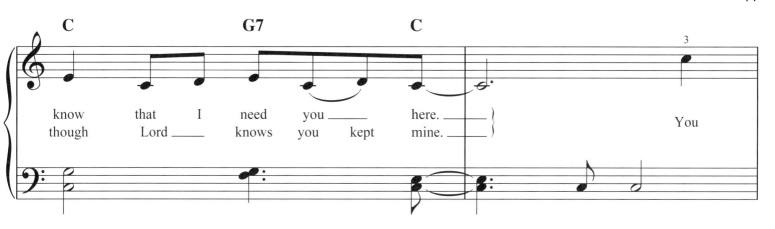

know that I need you _____ here. _____ You
though Lord _____ knows you kept _____ mine. _____

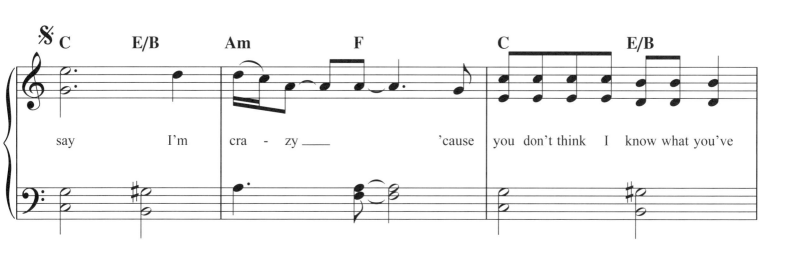

say I'm cra - zy _____ 'cause you don't think I know what you've

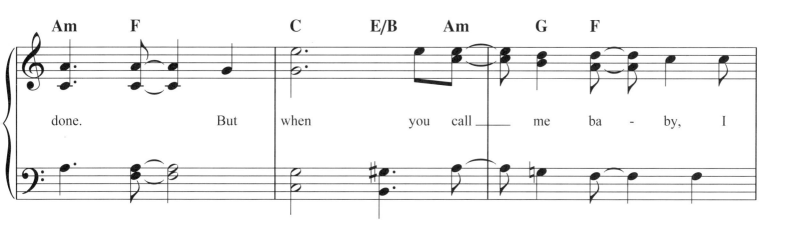

done. But when you call _____ me ba - by, I

To Coda ✪

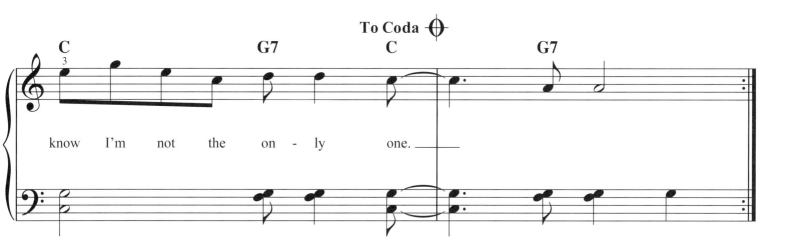

know I'm not the on - ly one. _____

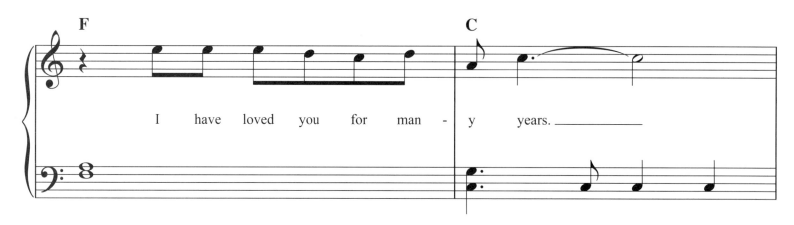

I have loved you for man - y years. _____

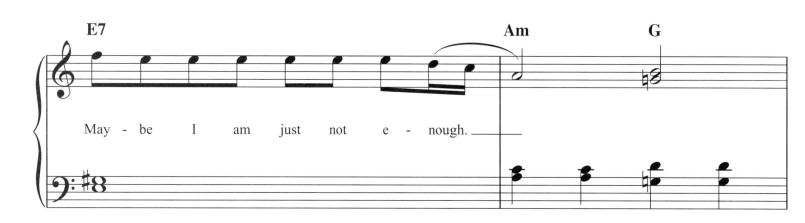

May - be I am just not e - nough. _____

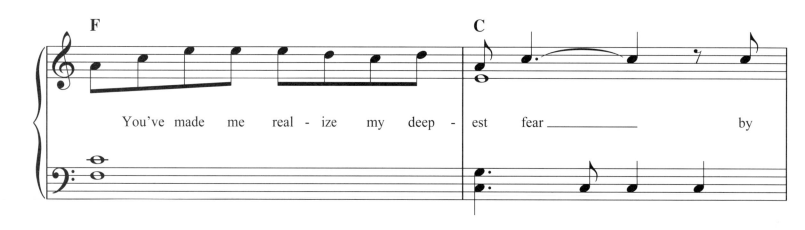

You've made me real - ize my deep - est fear _____ by

ly - ing and tear - ing us up. ____ You

CODA

HEARTBEAT SONG

Words and Music by JASON EVIGAN,
MITCH ALLAN, KARA DioGUARDI
and AUDRA MAE

Moderately fast

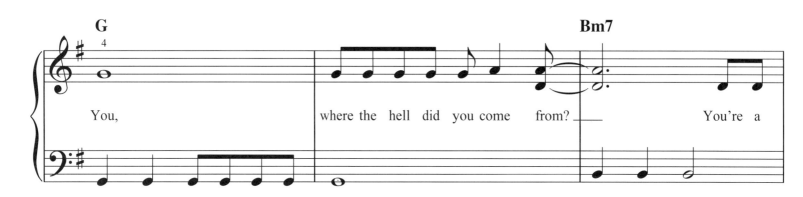

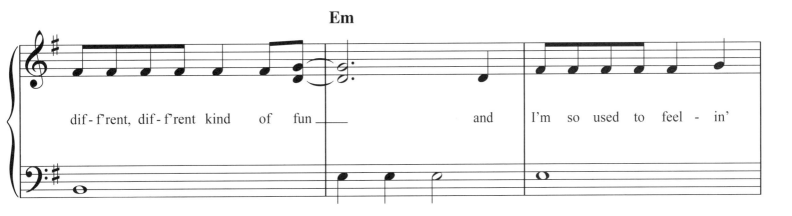

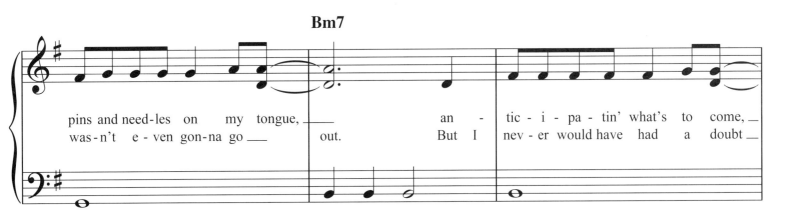

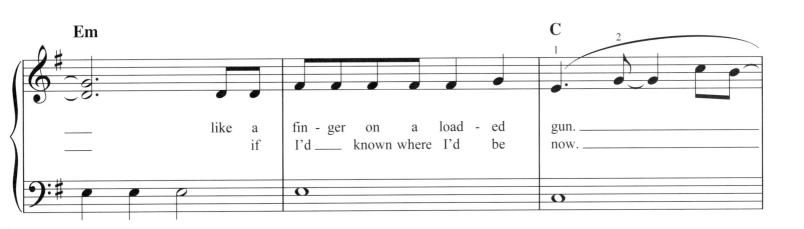

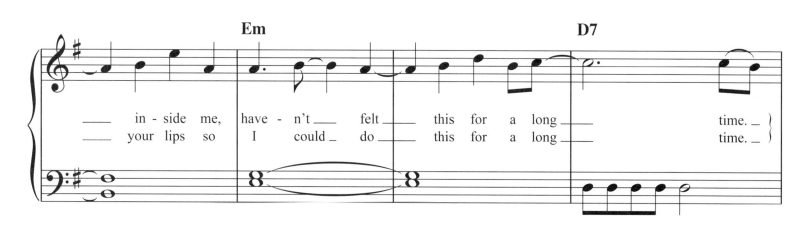

all night long, oh up, __ up all __ night long. __ This is my heart-

- beat song __ and I'm __ gon - na play __ it. Turned it on, but I know __

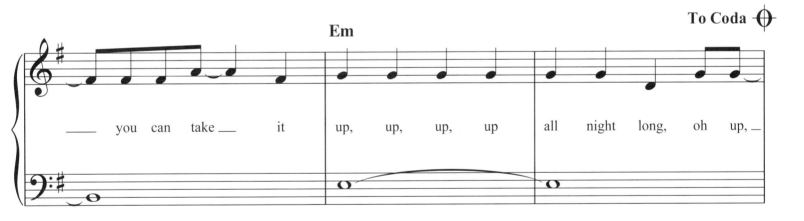

__ you can take __ it up, up, up, up all night long, oh up, __

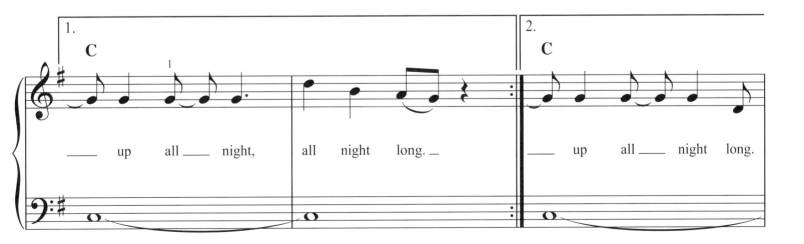

1.
__ up all __ night, all night long. __

2.
__ up all __ night long.

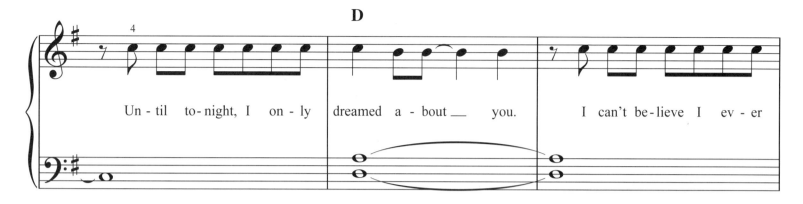

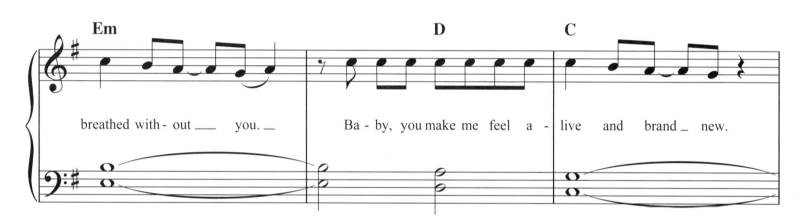

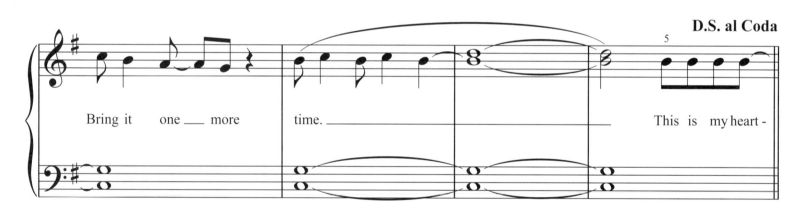

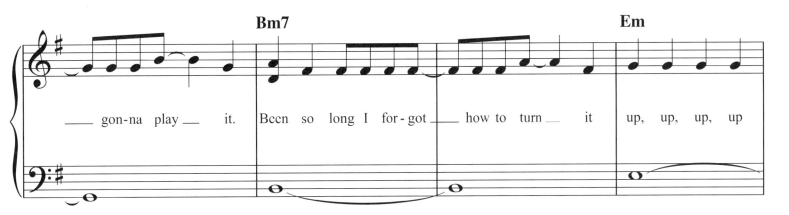

Bm7 ... **Em**

gon-na play ____ it. Been so long I for-got ____ how to turn ____ it up, up, up, up

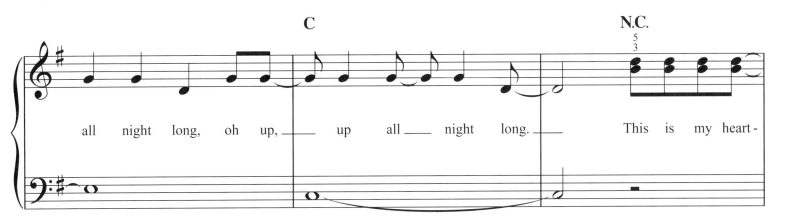

C ... **N.C.**

all night long, oh up, ____ up all ____ night long. ____ This is my heart-

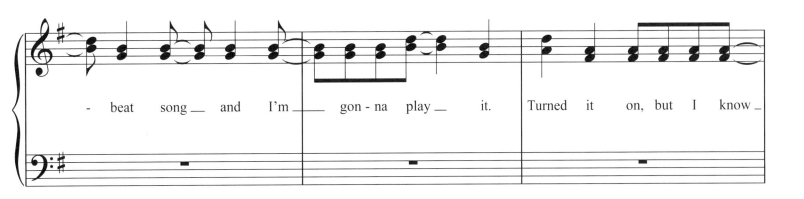

- beat song ____ and I'm ____ gon-na play ____ it. Turned it on, but I know ____

____ you can take ____ it up, up, up, up all night long, oh up, ____ up all ____ night long.

I REALLY LIKE YOU

Words and Music by CARLY RAE JEPSEN,
PETER SVENSSON and JACOB KASHER HINDLIN

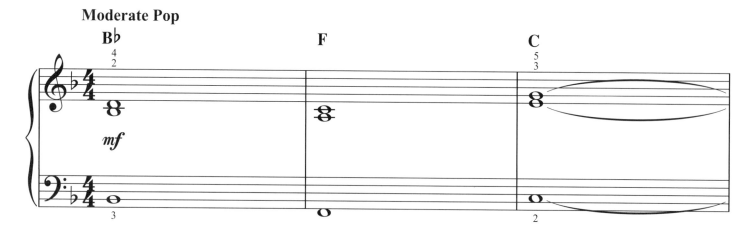

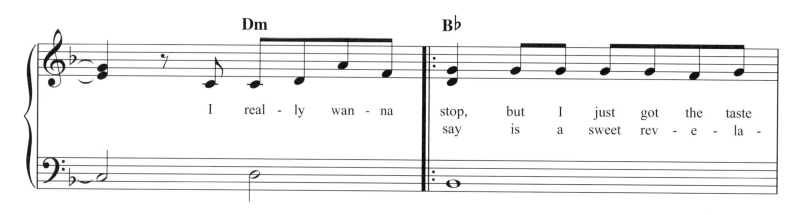

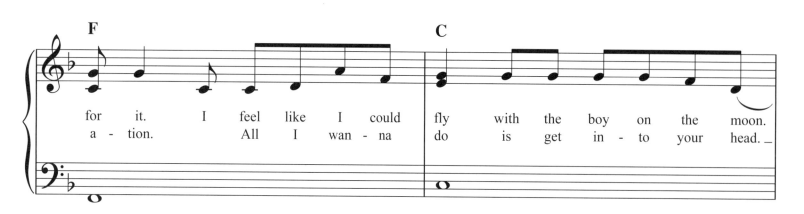

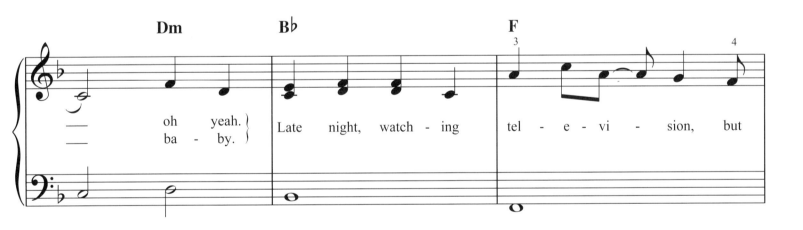

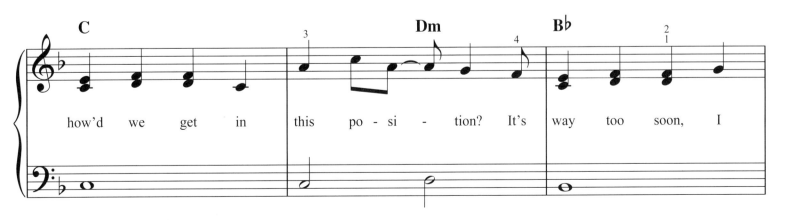

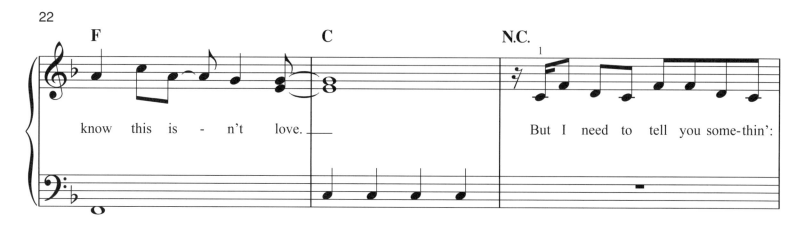

know this is - n't love. But I need to tell you some-thin':

I real - ly, real - ly, real - ly, real - ly, real - ly, real - ly like you, —

and I want you. Do you want me, do you want me too?

I real - ly, real - ly, real - ly, real - ly, real - ly, real - ly like you, —

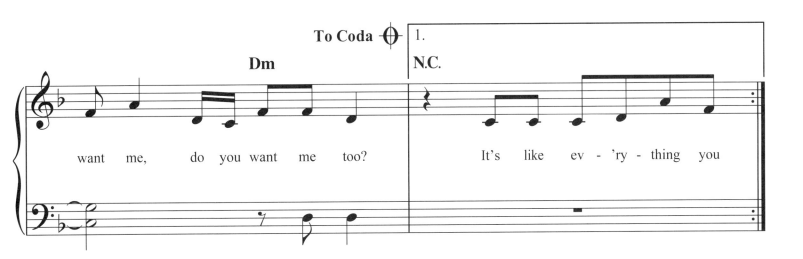

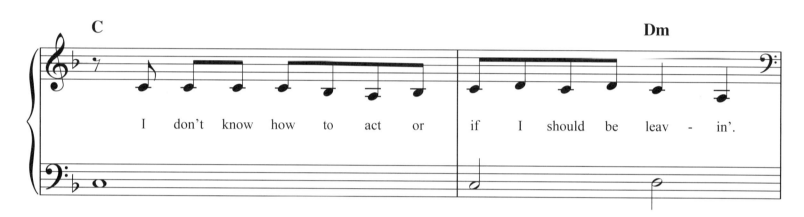

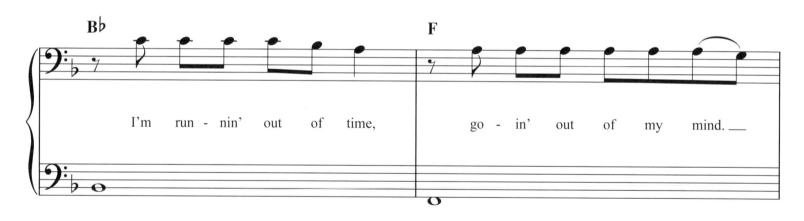

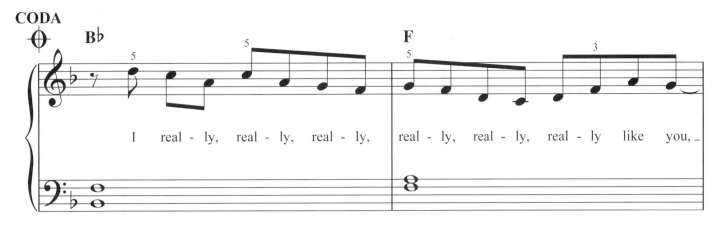

THINKING OUT LOUD

Words and Music by ED SHEERAN
and AMY WADGE

Slowly

When your legs don't work like they used to be-fore
When my hair's all gone and my mem-o-ry fades

and I can't sweep you off of your feet,
and the crowds don't re-mem-ber my name.

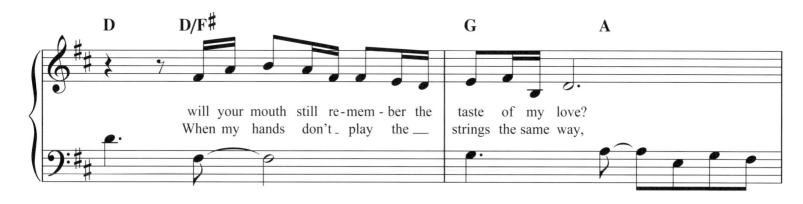

will your mouth still re-mem-ber the taste of my love?
When my hands don't play the strings the same way,

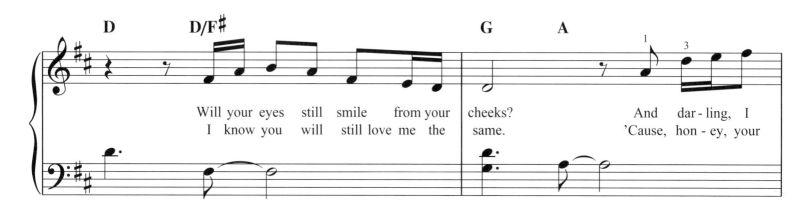

Will your eyes still smile from your cheeks? And dar-ling, I
I know you will still love me the same. 'Cause, hon-ey, your

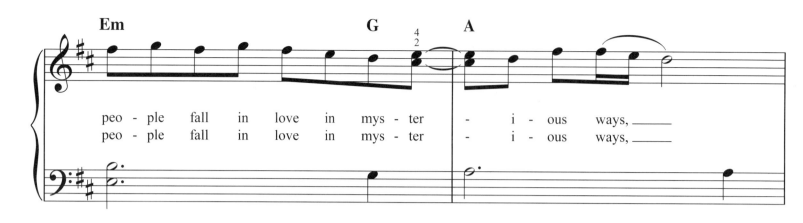

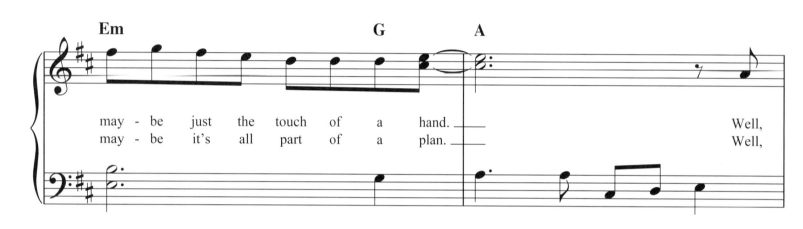

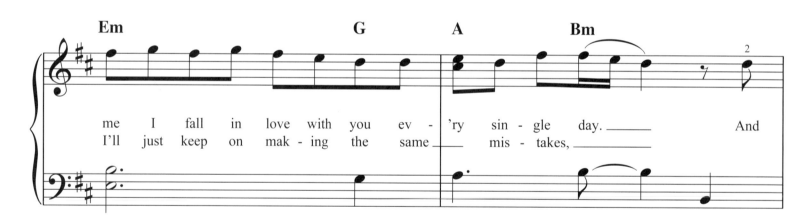

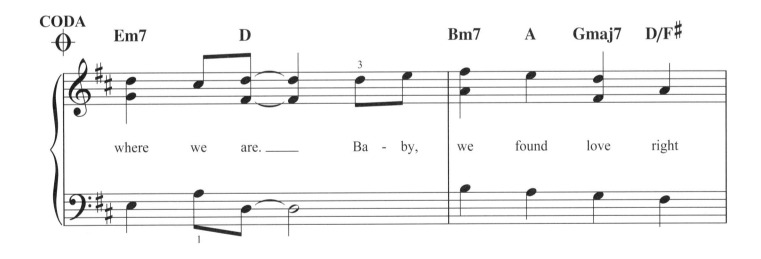

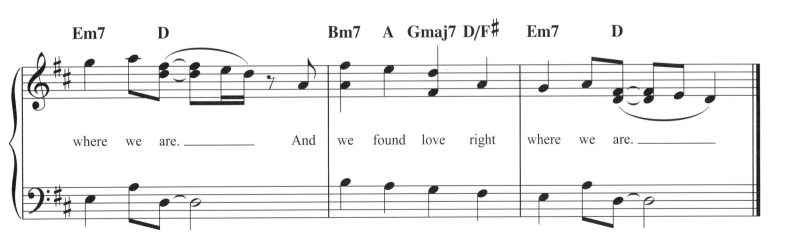

POP PIANO HITS

Pop Piano Hits is a series designed for students of all ages. Each book contains five simple and easy-to-read arrangements of today's most popular downloads. Lyrics, fingering and chord symbols are included to help you make the most of each arrangement. Enjoy your favorite songs and artists today!

BLANK SPACE, I REALLY LIKE YOU & MORE HOT SINGLES
Blank Space (Taylor Swift) • Heartbeat Song (Kelly Clarkson) • I Really Like You (Carly Rae Jepsen) • I'm Not the Only One (Sam Smith) • Thinking Out Loud (Ed Sheeran).
00146286 Easy Piano $9.99

CALL ME MAYBE, HOME & MORE HOT SINGLES
Call Me Maybe (Carly Rae Jepsen) • Heart Attack (Demi Lovato) • Home (Phillip Phillips) • Just Give Me a Reason (Pink) • Next to Me (Emeli Sandé).
00121544 Easy Piano $9.99

GET LUCKY, BLURRED LINES & MORE HOT SINGLES
Blurred Lines (Robin Thicke feat. T.I. + Pharrell) • Brave (Sara Bareilles) • Cruise (Florida Georgia Line) • Cups (When I'm Gone) (Anna Kendrick) • Get Lucky (Daft Punk feat. Pharrell Williams).
00122334 Easy Piano $9.99

HO HEY, SOME NIGHTS & MORE HOT SINGLES
Ho Hey (The Lumineers) • It's Time (Imagine Dragons) • Some Nights (fun.) • Stay (Rihanna) • When I Was Your Man (Bruno Mars).
00119861 Easy Piano $9.99

LET IT GO, HAPPY & MORE HOT SINGLES
All of Me (John Legend) • Dark Horse (Katy Perry) • Happy (Pharrell) • Let It Go (Demi Lovato) • Pompeii (Bastille).
00128204 Easy Piano $9.99

ROAR, ROYALS & MORE HOT SINGLES
Atlas (Coldplay – from *The Hunger Games: Catching Fire*) • Roar (Katy Perry) • Royals (Lorde) • Safe and Sound (Capital Cities) • Wake Me Up! (Avicii).
00123868 Easy Piano $9.99

SAY SOMETHING, COUNTING STARS & MORE HOT SINGLES
Counting Stars (One Republic) • Demons (Imagine Dragons) • Let Her Go (Passenger) • Say Something (A Great Big World) • Story of My Life (One Direction).
00125356 Easy Piano $9.99

SHAKE IT OFF, ALL ABOUT THAT BASS & MORE HOT SINGLES
All About That Bass (Meghan Trainor) • Shake It Off (Taylor Swift) • A Sky Full of Stars (Coldplay) • Something in the Water (Carrie Underwood) • Take Me to Church (Hozier).
00142734 Easy Piano $9.99

STAY WITH ME, SING & MORE HOT SINGLES
Am I Wrong? (Nico & Vinz) • Boom Clap (from *The Fault in Our Stars*) (Charli XCX) • Love Runs Out (One Republic) • Sing (Ed Sheeran) • Stay with Me (Sam Smith).
00138067 Easy Piano $9.99

Prices, contents and availability subject to change without notice.

HAL•LEONARD® CORPORATION
7777 W. BLUEMOUND RD. P.O. BOX 13819 MILWAUKEE, WI 53213

www.halleonard.com

0415